echoes of love

esther roseglenn

isbn: 979-8-9987525-4-4

published by glenn & rose publishing

printed in the united states of america

first edition

for my parents, glenn and rosita
your love shaped my world,
and your absence gave these pages their voice.

to my husband, george
thank you for being my anchor, my quiet strength,
and the one who holds steady when the waves come.

to my sister, stephanie
my fiercest protector, and the one who has shared this grief
in the only way a sister and best friend could.

to my md girls and my dearest friends
thank you for your continued presence,
and for showing me that grief is lighter when shared.

and to anyone carrying a grief that words can't fully hold
may you feel seen, comforted, and never alone.

dear grieving heart,

if you're here, something has shifted in your world,
and not by choice.
i'm so sorry.

as the world keeps moving in its familiar rhythms,
you're left in a reality that feels different.
this is for you.

in the pages ahead, you'll find 100 reflections,
honest, sometimes heartbreakingly so.
words for the multitude of feelings
that rise when we're asked to keep going.

these began as quiet thoughts i told myself
on days when everything felt too heavy to name.
over time, they became companions,
reminders that even the hardest days
deserve softness and space.

some may bring comfort. others may be hard to hold.
you're allowed to pause, to skip, to return later.

there's no right way to move through this book.
read it in pieces, or let it rest beside you.

this is not a guide or a roadmap.
it's a quiet presence.
the kind that simply says,
you're not alone.

your friend in grief,
esther

the ache

grief arrives like a storm you never saw coming.
it shakes everything you once knew
and leaves you standing in the wreckage,
breathless and bewildered.

it is the first shatter of what once felt whole.
the place where love feels like pain.

there's no guidebook for the weight
you now carry.
some days it's sharp.
some days it's numb.
some days it's both.

this section is here for those first, raw emotions.
the shock, the anger, the disbelief,
the unbearable missing.

there are no right or wrong feelings here.
only the simple truth:
you are grieving, and you are allowed
to feel all of it.
you don't have to weather this alone.

sometimes grief feels like
the ground has disappeared beneath you.
you reach out,
but there's nothing to hold onto.
only the empty space where someone once stood.

some mornings you may
wake up and forget for a second.
then the weight returns,
like a shadow
stitched into your bones.

it can feel
like walking through fog.
disorienting, heavy, relentless.
still, you keep going.

there are days
when even breathing feels like effort.
exhaustion settles in your bones,
and getting through the day
is the bravest thing you'll do.

grief rewires
the way you wait for life.
even in the quiet,
you scan for shadows
as if something might break again.

you may feel like you're floating
outside your own life,
watching yourself
go through the motions
with a heart that no longer fits.

grief is not polite.
it appears in the middle
of conversations, errands, and quiet moments.
it's the uninvited guest
who never leaves.

grief can bring anger
that surprises you.
at the unfairness,
at the finality,
at how the world keeps spinning.
it's not wrong to feel it.
it means you cared deeply.

there are days
when nothing feels right.
not your body,
not the air,
not the world without them.

it's okay if you don't have
the energy to explain your pain.
grief speaks a language
that often feels impossible
to translate.

there will be days
when the tears won't come,
even when you need them to.
the quiet can carry its own kind of pain.

sometimes the hardest part
is how the world forgets
what you still remember
every single day.

there are still days
when it doesn't feel real.
you know they're gone,
but part of you
refuses to believe it.

you will ache
for what cannot return.
and sometimes,
for who you were
before everything changed.

grief can feel
like learning to live
in a life you didn't choose.
inhabiting a version of yourself
you're still trying to understand.

i used to know who i was.
now i look in the mirror
and search for someone
who still makes sense
in a world without them.

your heart might feel
both full and empty.
a memory can swell with love
in the same breath
it breaks with missing.
grief holds space for both.

you may question
if it's okay to laugh again.
as if joy has to ask
grief for permission.

things that once brought you comfort
now feel far away.
grief doesn't just take who you love.
it takes the warmth
they brought with them.

this is the hum
of love continuing
with nowhere to land.
it finds its way
in tears, in silence, in memory.

no one prepares you
for the weight of absence.
how heavy nothing feels
when it's the shape
of someone you love.

there is no wrong way to grieve.
some days you might feel distant from the pain.
on others, it may flood in all at once.
both are valid.

some pains
don't leave bruises.
grief sits beneath the skin,
tender to the touch
even when no one can see it.

you get good at wearing the mask,
smiling so no one has to worry.
you keep their comfort intact
while your own quietly breaks.
but just because you carry it well
doesn't mean it's not heavy.

you are allowed
to sit here in the ache.
there is no rush to move beyond it.

the silence

this is the silence
after the storm.
where the sharp edges soften,
but the absence grows louder.

it is the quiet
that follows the shatter.
a stillness
that hums with memory,
that aches without sound.

here, the world keeps turning,
but time feels suspended.
you are awake
in a place no one else sees.
the early mornings,
the long nights,
the pause between breaths.

this is where grief
sits beside reflection.
where questions surface,
and answers feel far away.

be here, as you are.
to let the hush hold you.
to listen for what remains
in the quiet
that only love could leave behind.

grief slows your world
while everything else keeps going.
the sun rises,
traffic moves,
people laugh
as if nothing has changed.
but everything has.
at least for you.

the quiet is loudest
when you face a choice
they would've helped you make.
their absence
echoes in uncertainty.

grief can feel
like forgetting how to be
in a room full of people.
present in body,
absent in spirit.

you pull away sometimes,
not because you want to be alone,
but because the world feels too loud
for the quiet you're still carrying.

there's a strange quiet
after the condolences stop.
the world resumes,
but your world
is still in pieces.

grief lingers
in the undone things.
the voicemail you can't delete,
the birthday card
you never got to send.

you might reread their texts
just to hear their voice in your mind.
even words on a screen
can feel like
a conversation with memory.

loss isn't always loud.
sometimes, it's the quiet
after you say their name
and no one answers.

you learn to carry the quiet,
not as emptiness,
but as a sacred space
where their memory lingers.

the silence doesn't just surround you.
it settles in you.
it changes how you move,
how you listen,
how you breathe.

grief changes the way
you hear the world.
familiar songs feel softer.
laughter lands heavier.
even ordinary sounds
don't sound the same.

grief makes you a keeper
of moments no one else remembers.
you carry their stories,
their laughter,
like fragile glass.

you may find comfort one day,
only to feel lost the next.
that's not a failure.
that's the rhythm of grief.

grief can live
in unfinished sentences,
unsaid goodbyes,
and the space between
what was and what will never be.

you learn to listen
for the places
where their presence used to be.
in pauses,
in breath,
in what isn't spoken anymore.

sometimes the most honest moments
happen when no one is around.
when the tears fall freely,
and silence
is the only witness.

some memories come gently,
like a whisper.
others arrive loudly,
then leave you
in stunned quiet.

you learn to sit
with unanswered questions,
to let them be part
of the new landscape
grief leaves behind.

grief doesn't announce itself.
it shows up in small things.
in the way the light falls through the window,
or in the quiet
that suddenly feels heavier than it should.

milestones arrive
and the room feels incomplete.
no voice cheering.
no hug waiting.
just a silence that knows what's missing.

you are not behind.
you are not doing it wrong.
the quiet just takes longer
to move through
than we're told it will.

sometimes, the silence feels soft.
a small relief in a restless world.
then comes the guilt
for finding any comfort where they are not.

you can still feel lost
even after you've "accepted" the loss.
grief isn't linear.
it's a landscape
you learn to live within.

it's okay to feel numb.
grief speaks in many languages,
and silence
is one of them.

if all you do today
is breathe through the quiet,
that is enough.
that is everything.

the longing

even in stillness,
grief keeps moving.

silence can give way to longing.
the yearning for what could have been,
for the future you imagined,
for one more conversation,
one more hug.

it feels like carrying
an invisible thread,
still tethered to someone
just out of reach.

the place where the heart
reaches for what's no longer here.

this is where grief settles into your bones,
where the weight of missing them
becomes a steady companion.

this section holds space
for the ache of longing,
the unanswered questions,
and the memories that linger.

here, you are invited
to honor both the sorrow
and the deep love that lives beneath it.

some days,
you'll long for what cannot return.
on others,
you'll miss the version of you
who existed when they were still here.

grief doesn't only miss the past.
it mourns the future, too.
the birthdays not celebrated,
the milestones not witnessed.

you might imagine
how they would respond
to your life now.
what they'd say,
how they'd laugh.
this imagining is a form of love.

grief brings with it
a craving for familiarity.
not for the world to move on,
but to go back
to how it used to be.

missing someone
isn't just about the big things.
it's the coffee cup,
the shared glance,
the absence woven into routine.

grief can make time feel cruel.
you watch the calendar move forward,
but part of you
is still standing in that one
life-changing moment.

you may find yourself
laughing, then crying.
because you wanted
to share that joy
with the person who's gone.

your hands still reach
for theirs sometimes.
in dreams,
in memories,
in muscle memory.

longing can be
the heaviness
that greets you each morning.
before memory fully arrives,
but after you know they're gone.

some nights,
you'll dream they're still here.
and for a moment,
you'll forget they're gone.
waking feels like losing them all over again.

you can be surrounded
by love and still miss
the way they saw you.
like they held a version of you
no one else quite knew.

grief can turn into longing
for things you never got to say,
for moments that only existed
in the future
you were supposed to have.

sometimes, it catches you off guard.
a scent, a song, a familiar sky.
and suddenly, they're here again.
not in the way they once were,
but in a way love allows:
quiet, lasting, still yours.

your body still reaches
for what your heart remembers.
not out of pain,
but out of a love
that hasn't found a new place to land.

some days you don't want advice.
you want the person
who would just know.
who understood the parts of you
that didn't need fixing.

you may find yourself
reaching for your phone,
to share the news,
to hear their voice.
then you remember,
they're not on the other end anymore.

grief can make old joys
feel foreign.
what once lit you up
now flickers.
not gone, just changed.

some nights,
you may whisper into the quiet,
hoping that somewhere
they still hear you.

some memories return as words.
you replay them,
listening for what was unsaid,
wondering what you missed,
and what you'd say
if time let you try again.

there is a kind of loneliness
that only comes
from missing someone
who felt like home.

you find yourself
replaying the same moment
over and over.
not because it brings comfort,
but because any memory
is better than letting go.

there's a space in joy
only they could fill.
even in happiness,
you notice the outline
of their absence.

sometimes the hardest part
is not what happened,
but what didn't.
the wedding they missed.
the child they'll never meet.

longing teaches you
how deep love can reach.
so deep,
it lingers
even when there's no one left to hold.

longing isn't always painful.
sometimes,
it's the tender reminder
that love didn't end
just because they're gone.

the love that remains

grief may one day invite us
to carry love alongside loss.

the sharp edges soften,
and in their place
is a quiet remembering.
a way to honor
the life that touched yours
so deeply.

this is the space for enduring love.
the legacy that lingers,
the warmth that memory can bring
when it doesn't hurt quite as much.

here, you'll find words
for the quiet strength
that grows in the space
where grief and love meet.

this is where remembering becomes ritual,
where the ache makes room
for tenderness,
and the love that stays
quietly reshapes everything.

love doesn't end when someone is gone.
it continues in how you speak of them,
how you carry them forward,
how you live with the space
they once filled.

grief can turn ordinary places
into sacred ground.
a chair.
a coat.
the way the light used to fall
when they were still here.

you don't owe anyone closure.
some stories remain open.
not because they're unfinished,
but because love like this
doesn't need an ending.

let yourself honor them
in ways that feel natural.
a journal entry.
a walk.
a whispered hello.
these moments matter.

sometimes their presence returns
in the smallest ways.
a phrase, a kindness,
a moment of peace
you can't quite explain.

you can still talk to them.
in the car.
under your breath.
in the silence of morning.
some conversations don't need replies.

you didn't need to be ready
for the goodbye to matter.
the love was enough.
it still is.

you may find yourself laughing again,
and then feeling guilty for it.
but joy does not erase grief.
it grows beside it.

you don't have to feel better
to keep living.
some days are soft,
some aren't.
both count.

even in your quietest moments,
you are surrounded
by the echoes of being loved.
not loud,
but still steady.

you can miss them
without searching for signs.
some days, absence is the whole thing,
and that's okay.

this isn't the life you imagined.
but here you are.
still loving, still remembering,
still finding ways to live inside the after.

some memories return easily.
others fade.
you don't have to hold on tightly
for love to still be real.

grief doesn't ask you to move on.
just to keep moving,
with your heart intact
and your love unchanged.

some days will pass
without a single thought of them.
that's okay.
love doesn't disappear
just because it grows quieter.

there will be days
you forget to grieve.
that doesn't mean you've forgotten.
it means you are learning to live again.

even when no one else brings them up,
you're allowed to.
their name still matters.
their story still lives.

joy might return differently.
quieter, slower.
you don't have to chase it.
it will find its way back to you.

not everything has to be healed.
some love lives beside the loss.
unresolved,
but whole
in its own quiet way.

it's okay if their voice feels distant now,
or if their scent has slipped from memory.
missing these things
doesn't mean you loved them any less.
it just means time has passed.
let the ache of forgetting
be part of your remembering, too.

there's no timeline for remembering.
you might cry ten years from now
over something small.
that, too, is love showing up
without warning.

they're not here
to see your days unfold,
but sometimes, without trying,
you find yourself living
in ways that feel like them.

you are proof
that their love existed.
that it mattered.
that it still does.

love is not erased by time.
if anything, it deepens.
quietly,
and often when you least expect it.

the love that remains
will meet you again and again
in stillness,
in longing,
in laughter,
in life.
let it.

dear friend in grief,

thank you for spending time in this space.
whether you read one reflection or many,
i hope these words offered gentleness
and quiet company.

this book is not here to solve grief.
it's here to sit with it.
to hold space for the ache, the silence,
the longing, and the love that remains.

these reflections are meant to be
returned to gently.
they are echoes of love,
soft reminders that you are
not alone in what you carry.

you have walked through more than words can hold.
and still, you are here.

grief moves in waves, reshaping itself with time.
it lingers through seasons, and across quiet years.
these pages will be here whenever you need them.
a quiet place to land.

from my grieving heart to yours,

esther

www.ingramcontent.com/pod-product-compliance
Lightning Source LLC
Chambersburg PA
CBHW030548130626
46552CB00006B/2478